The Bridals by Margaret Cavendish

Margaret Lucas Cavendish, Duchess of Newcastle-upon-Tyne was born in 1623 in Colchester, Essex into a family of comfortable means.

As the youngest of eight children she spent much time with her siblings. Margaret had no formal education but she did have access to scholarly libraries and tutors, although she later said the children paid little attention to the tutors, who were there 'rather for formality than benefit'.

From an early age Margaret was already assembling her thoughts for future works despite the then conditions of society that women did not partake in public authorship. For England it was also a time of Civil War. The Royalists were being pushed back and Parliamentary forces were in the ascendancy.

Despite these obvious dangers, when Queen Henrietta Maria was in Oxford, Margaret asked her mother for permission to become one of her Ladies-in-waiting. She was accepted and, in 1644, accompanied the Queen into exile in France. This took her away from her family for the first time.

Despite living at the Court of the young King Louis XIV, life for the young Margaret was not what she expected. She was far from her home and her confidence had been replaced by shyness and difficulties fitting in to the grandeur of her surroundings and the eminence of her company.

Margaret told her mother she wanted to leave the Court. Her mother was adamant that she should stay and not disgrace herself by leaving. She provided additional funds for her to make life easier. Margaret remained. It was now also that she met and married William Cavendish who, at the time, was the Marquis of Newcastle (and later Duke). He was also 30 years her senior and previously married with two children.

As Royalists, a return to life in England was not yet possible. They would remain in exile in Paris, Rotterdam and Antwerp until the restoration of the crown in 1660 although Margaret was able to return for attention to some estate matters.

Along with her husband's brother, Sir Charles Cavendish, she travelled to England after having been told that her husband's estate (taken from him due to his being a royalist) was to be sold and that she, as his wife, would receive some benefit of the sale. She received nothing. She left England to be with her husband again.

The couple were devoted to each other. Margaret wrote that he was the only man she was ever in love with, loving him not for title, wealth or power, but for merit, justice, gratitude, duty, and fidelity. She also relied upon him for support in her career. The marriage provided no children despite efforts made by her physician to overcome her inability to conceive.

Margaret's first book, 'Poems and Fancies', was published in 1653; it was a collection of poems, epistles and prose pieces which explores her philosophical, scientific and aesthetic ideas.

For a woman at this time writing and publishing were avenues they had great difficulty in pursuing. Added to this was Margaret's range of subjects. She wrote across a number of issues including gender, power, manners, scientific method, and philosophy.

She always claimed she had too much time on her hands and was therefore able to indulge her love of writing. As a playwright she produced many works although most are as closet dramas. (This is a play not intended to be performed onstage, but instead read by a solitary reader or perhaps out loud in a small group. For Margaret the rigours of exile, her gender and Cromwell's closing of the theatres mean this was her early vehicle of choice and, despite these handicaps, she became one of the most well-known playwrights in England)

Her utopian romance, 'The Blazing World', (1666) is one of the earliest examples of science fiction. Margaret also published extensively in natural philosophy and early modern science; at least a dozen books.

She was the first woman to attend a meeting at Royal Society of London in 1667 and she criticized and engaged with members and philosophers Thomas Hobbes, René Descartes, and Robert Boyle.

Margaret was always defended against any criticism by her husband and he also contributed to some of her works. She also gives him credit as her writing tutor.

Perhaps a little strangely she said her ambition despite her shyness, was to have everlasting fame. During her career, from the mid 1650's until her death, she was prolific. In recent decades her work has undergone a resurgence of interest propelled mainly by her ground-breaking attitude and accomplishments in those male straitened times.

Margaret Cavendish died on 15th December 1673 and was buried at Westminster Abbey.

Index of Contents

THE BRIDALS

THE CAST LIST
Monsieur Take-Pleasure, Brideman
Monsieur Adviser, Brideman
Monsieur Facil. Brideman
Monsieur Courtly. Brideman
Master Longlife
Master Aged
Sir Mercury Poet, and the Lady Fancy his Bride
Sir William Sage, and the Lady Vertue his Bride
Sir John Amorous, and the Lady Coy his Bride
Madam Mediator. And other Ladies
Mimick the Fool
Joan, a Cook-maid

ACT I

SCENE I

[Enter **MONSIEUR TAKE-PLEASURE** and **MONSIEUR ADVISER**, and meet **MONSIEUR FACIL.**

MONSIEUR ADVISER
Facil,
Where have you been so early this morning, abroad?

MONSIEUR FACIL
I have been at Church, to see a young Virgin and a Batchellor married to day.

MONSIEUR TAKE-PLEASURE
How do you know she is a Virgin?

MONSIEUR FACIL
By her modest Countenance.

MONSIEUR TAKE-PLEASURE
Faith, Women have more modesty in their countenance, then in their natures; wherefore you may be deceived by her countenance; for Womens countenances, like false glasses, make their minds appear fairer then they are; for a modest countenance may have a wanton mind.

MONSIEUR FACIL
But this Brides countenance was so modest,
I wish that I had been her Bridegroom.

MONSIEUR ADVISER
Would you have married her only for her modest countenance?

MONSIEUR FACIL
Yes, for a modest countenance is the greatest
Beauty in my eye.

MONSIEUR ADVISER
Faith, that Beauty never lasts above a day, nay, an hours acquaintance fadeth it, two hours wither it, and in three hours it is quite vanish'd away.

MONSIEUR FACIL
Some Women have modest countenances and natures all their life-time.

MONSIEUR ADVISER
Their life must be very short, if it last no longer then their modesty: 'Tis true, Women have feigned modesty, but not real modesty; for they put on modesty, as they do paint, the one to make them appear fairer, the other to make them appear chaster then they are.

MONSIEUR FACIL
You do not deserve either a modest, or chast Woman.

MONSIEUR ADVISER
Faith, I hate both modesty and chastity in Women; for modesty and chastity are enemies to the Masculine Sex, and worse then a Cloister, as being more restraint.

MONSIEUR FACIL
Well, leaving Modesty, Chastity and Cloisters, will you go to the Bridal-House?

MONSIEUR ADVISER
Yes, for I believe there will be liberty and choice.

MONSIEUR FACIL
There will be two choice Brides.

MONSIEUR TAKE-PLEASURE
Why, hath one Man married two Women?

MONSIEUR FACIL
No, but two Men have married two Women; for there are two Brides and two Bridegrooms.

MONSIEUR ADVISER
It had been better that one Bridegroom had two Brides, for then he might have spar'd one for a Friend.

MONSIEUR FACIL
It had not been better for you, unless you had been that Friend to receive that Courtesie.

MONSIEUR TAKE-PLEASURE
I would have endeavour'd with all the Rhetorick I have, and all the Protestations I could make, and all the Oaths I could swear, to make him believe I was his Friend, that he might be my Friend.

MONSIEUR FACIL
Come, come, they would have done thee no service.

MONSIEUR ADVISER
But I might have done him service, at least to his spare-Bride; but who are those that are Married?

MONSIEUR FACIL
Sir John Amorous, to the Lady Coy; and Sir William Sage, to the Lady Vertue.

[Exeunt.

[Enter **MR LONG-LIFE**, and **MR AGED**.

MR AGED
Mr. Longlife, I am glad to see you look so well, and that you are strong and lusty.

MR LONG-LIFE
So am I to see you so, good Master Aged.

MR AGED
I thank God, though I am old, I feel no stitches.

MR LONG-LIFE
Beshrew me, I feel some stitches now and then

MR AGED
O! that is nothing, for the youngest and strongest Man of them all, will feel stitches sometimes.

MR LONG-LIFE
I rather wish the young Men did feel them, then I, for they are better able to endure them; but what News do you hear Mr. Aged?

MR AGED
Faith, none that is good, or that is worth the hearing.

MR LONG-LIFE

It is a sign the times are bad, the times are bad.

MR AGED

Men are so evil, Mr. Longlife, that the times must needs be so.

MR LONG-LIFE

The times were better when we were young.

MR AGED

We thought them so, being young; for young Men have not much experience, nor long acquaintance of the World; they endeavour to know, and be acquainted with the Vices in the VVorld, though not the Vertues.

MR LONG-LIFE

Faith, Vertue is rather talked of, then known, at least then practised.

MR AGED

Indeed Men preach Vertue, but practise Vice.

MR LONG-LIFE

'Tis such old Men as we are, that are the Preachers, and young Men the Practitioners.

MR AGED

Yes, evil young Men say,
That old Men preach Vertue, when they are past practising Vice.

MR LONG-LIFE

Indeed young Men despise old Men's Counsels and Advice, and will believe nothing they say, untill they live to be old themselves, and then they see their past-follies, and think themselves only wise, because they are old.

MR AGED

Then all Men think themselves wise, if young Men think themselves wiser then old Men, and old Men think themselves wiser then young Men.

MR LONG-LIFE

'Tis true, they do so; and the same way Men think other Men Fools; for young Men think old Men Fools, and old Men think young Men Fools.

MR AGED

Nay, old Men do more then think young Men Fools, for they know young Men are Fools; for 'tis impossible they can be wise, for wisdom is not born with Men, nor left to Men as Inheritances are.

MR LONG-LIFE

No By'rlady, they must be bound Apprentices to Time, and serve Time many years, before they can be wise Men.

MR AGED
Well, let us leave foolish young Men to Time, and let you and I go take the fresh air for Health.

MR LONG-LIFE
With all my heart, let us go.

[Exeunt.

[Enter the **BRIDES** and **BRIDEGROOMS**, and all the **BRIDAL GUESTS**, **SIR MERCURY POET** one of the Bride-Men, and the **LADY FANCY** one of the Bride-Maids, that helps to lead one of the Brides to the Church.

MONSIEUR ADVISER
Gentlemen Bridegrooms, we must rifle your Brides of their Bride-Garters.

SIR JOHN AMOROUS
If it be the custom, I submit.

SIR WILLIAM SAGE
But I will not agree to such an uncivil custom, for no man shall pull off my Wives Garters, unless it be my self.

LADY VERTUE
We have pull'd off our Garters already, and therefore if these Batchellor-Gentlemen, will have them, we will send for them.

MONSIEUR FACIL
Pray Ladies let us have them, for the Bride-Garters are the young Batchellors fees.

MONSIEUR COURTLY
Since we must not rifle for their Garters, let us cast Dice for them.

MONSIEUR TAKE-PLEASURE
Content.

MADAM MEDIATOR
The Bridegrooms points being our fees, therefore we must rifle for the points.

SIR WILLIAM SAGE
If you please Ladies, we are ready to be rifled.

[The **WOMEN** offer to take off the Points, but **LADY VERTUE** hinders them.

LADY VERTUE
Ladies, pray stay, for it is the custom, not to unpoint the Bridegrooms, until they be ready to go to bed.

SIR WILLIAM SAGE
I am ready to go to Bed, if the Ladies please.

ONE OF THE FEMALE GUESTS
No, we will stay till Night.

[Exeunt all, but **TWO OF THE LADIES**.

1ST LADY
The Lady Coy is one of the most modest and bashful Brides that ever I saw; in so much, as she is ashamed to look upon her Bridegroom.

2ND LADY
Some of her modesty ought to be reserved, or else she will have none left for to morrow.

1ST LADY
Why, doth Modesty wast like a Watch-candle, in a night?

2ND LADY
Yes, faith, it is a light that soon goes out, or rather a shadow that soon vanishes.

1ST LADY
Then the Lady Vertue has no shadows, for she appears neither bashful, nor bold; but she is both in her Behaviour and Countenance like a Bridal-Guest, rather then a Bride.

[Exeunt.

SCENE II

[Enter the **BRIDES**, **BRIDEGROOMS**, and all their **BRIDAL-GUESTS**, **MEN** and **WOMEN**.

SIR JOHN AMOROUS
Pray let us not dance, but go to bed.

MADAM MEDIATOR
That will be an injury to your Bridal-Guests, to rob them of their Mirth and Musick, by going to bed so soon.

LADY VERTUE
No, Ladies, we will dance; Musick, play.

[The Musick plays, and they dance; **SIR JOHN AMOROUS** kisses his **BRIDE**, and Courts her with smiles and amorous looks.

SIR WILLIAM SAGE
Gentlemen, and Ladies, for Heavens sake, have mercy upon two languishing Bridegrooms, and leave off dancing for this time.

MADAM MEDIATOR
Have I found you out, Sir William Sage!

SIR WILLIAM SAGE
I was never hid, Madam.

MADAM MEDIATOR
Yes, but you were; for now I perceive you would go to bed with your Bride.

SIR WILLIAM SAGE
I shall not need to obscure my desires, Madam, for it is lawful for any Man to lie with his own wife.

MADAM MEDIATOR
You are a Wag, you are a Wag, Sir William.

SIR WILLIAM SAGE
No Madam, for to be a Wag, is to be unseasonably wanton, which I am not.

SIR JOHN AMOROUS
Faith, this Dancing is unseasonable, therefore fair Ladies, attend the fair Brides to bed.

FEMALE GUESTS
Come, Lady Coy, we will help to undress you.

LADY COY
No truly, but you shall not, for I will not go to bed.

[They seem earnest to have her to bed, and she to stay.

SIR WILLIAM SAGE
What is the matter, Ladies, will not you let our Brides go to bed?

FEMALE GUESTS
We desire to wait on them, and to help to undress them, but the Lady Coy will not go to bed.

SIR WILLIAM SAGE
Then pray go with my Bride.

ONE OF THE LADIES
Yes, if she please to go to bed.

SIR WILLIAM SAGE
Wife will not you go to bed?

LADY VERTUE
Yes, if you please to have me.

SIR WILLIAM SAGE

'Tis my desire.

[Exit **LADY VERTUE**, and some of the **LADIES** with her: **SIR JOHN AMOROUS** comes and kisses his **BRIDE**.

SIR JOHN AMOROUS
Pray go to Bed.

LADY COY
Pray let me stay here.

MONSIEUR ADVISER
Faith, she would be carried to bed; carry your Wife to bed, Sir John Amorous.

SIR JOHN AMOROUS
Not against her will, although against her consent.

MONSIEUR ADVISER
In words you mean.

SIR JOHN AMOROUS
Come, Sweet-heart, I will usher you into your Chamber.

[Exit **SIR JOHN AMOROUS**, leading his **BRIDE**, who seems very unwilling to go, all the Company goeth with them, only **MONSIEUR ADVISER** and **MONSIEUR FACIL** stay; **MONSIEUR FACIL** fetches a sigh.

MONSIEUR FACIL
O how happy a man is Sir John Amorous! and how unhappy a man am I!

MONSIEUR ADVISER
Perchance two days hence, Sir J. Amorous will think himself as unhappy, as you think your self now, for a great surfeit is as bad as a sharp hunger.

[Exeunt.

SCENE III

[Enter the **LADY VERTUE** as in her Chamber, with some other **FEMALE GUESTS**; she seems to undress her self.

LADY VERTUE
Pray Ladies help to undress me.

MADAM MEDIATOR
That we will.

[They unpin her Gorget.

MADAM MEDIATOR
Shall we fling the Stockins when you and your Bridegroom are a bed?

LADY VERTUE
Yes, if you please, Ladies.

MADAM MEDIATOR
And shall we break the Bride-Cake over your head?

LADY VERTUE
I must intreat you to omit that custom, as also setting a Sack-posset upon the bed; for the crumbs of Cake and drops of Posset, will be very ill bed-fellows; besides, it is not a cleanly Custom; but I have given order that all such Junkets shall be provided for you in another room, to make you merry, when I and my Husband are a bed.

MADAM MEDIATOR
So I perceive, you will send us away, as soon as you can.

LADY VERTUE
I'le leave your staying, or going away, to your own discretion.

[Enter a **MAID-SEREVANT**.

SERVANT
Madam, your Bridegroom hath sent to know, whether you be in Bed.

LADY VERTUE
I shall be in a short time, tell him: Come Ladies, let us go into the Bed-chamber.

[Exeunt.

[Enter **SIR JOHN AMOROUS**, and his **BRIDE**, with the rest of the **FEMALE-GUESTS**.

SIR JOHN AMOROUS
Ladies, I shall leave my Bride with you, to help her to bed.

[Exit **SIR JOHN AMOROUS**.

MADAM MEDIATOR
Come, Lady Coy, to morrow you will be Lady Amorous.

1ST LADY
Why, do Wives never take their Husbands name till the day after Marriage?

MADAM MEDIATOR
No, for the first day, they neither are called by their own, nor their Husbands name; but are called Brides, as an Interlude between both.

2ND LADY
Come, come, undress the Bride.

MADAM MEDIATOR
That we will soon do.

LADY COY
I will not be undrest.

1ST LADY
What, Lady, will you lie in your Clothes?

MADAM MEDIATOR
If she will lie in her Clothes, it will neither be easie, convenient, nor cleanly; but come, come, Lady we will undress you.

[They offer to undress her, but she puts them back.

LADY COY
I will not be undrest.

MADAM MEDIATOR
Lady, give me leave to ask you, whether you married your Gown or your Person to your Husband?

LADY COY
My Person.

MADAM MEDIATOR
Then pull off your Gown, and go unclothed to bed.

LADY COY
I would undress me, but I am ashamed to lie with a Man.

MADAM MEDIATOR
That shame is very unnecessary at this time; wherefore cast it off with your Clothes.

LADY COY
I am afraid to lie by a Man.

MADAM MEDIATOR
That fear is an effeminate fear, and will not last long; wherefore undress, undress, for Loves sake.

LADY COY
I must go, and say my Prayers first.

MADAM MEDIATOR
Faith, Jove will dispence, with a Bride one night; the truth is, Bridal-Prayers are irreligious.

[Enter a **MAID** in hast.

MAID
Here comes the Bridegroom and all the Gentlemen attending him.

LADY COY
O! shut the door, shut the door, for Jupiters sake.

[The Scene to shut the door, the **MEN** knock.

MONSIEUR ADVISER
Open the Door, and let the Bridegroom in.

MADAM MEDIATOR
He cannot come as yet, the Bride's not a bed.

SIR JOHN AMOROUS
Let me come in, or I'le break open the door.

LADY COY
O keep him out, or I shall die for fear.

1ST LADY
You shall not come, until we please.

MONSIEUR FACIL
Let us come, or we will enter by force.

1ST LADY
You shall not, for we will defend the breach.

MONSIEUR COURTLY
With what? with what?

2ND LADY
With our Tongues and Armes.

MONSIEUR COURTLY
Your Tongues are pointless and edgless, and your Armes are weak defences.

MADAM MEDIATOR
You shall find them otherwise; but pray Sir J. Amorous carry away your unruly Regiment, and we will promise you upon our words, and honours, that as soon as the Bride is in Bed, we will come to you and give you notice, then usher you into the Bride-bed, with Epithalamiums.

SIR JOHN AMOROUS
Upon condition that you will be speedy, I will depart.

LADIES
We will, we will: Come Lady Coy to bed, to bed, for shame.

[Exeunt.

[Enter **SIR WILLIAM SAGE**, with all the **GENTLEMEN**, his **BRIDAL-GUESTS**, passing over the Stage, and going away again; after them comes **SIR JOHN AMOROUS**, as going to bed in his Night-Gown, **MADAM MEDIATOR** and the **LADIES** usher him, and when he passes, this Epithalamium is sung.

[Epithalamium.
Now at the Door
You'l stand no more,
But enter the Bridal-bed:
Where you will prove
The Sweets of Love
With God Hymen's banquet fed.
Then Noble Knight
Put out the Light,
Her flaming Eyes will guide you;
And in her Armes
Those Circled Charmes
In Wedlock's Islands hide you.
Now all the joyes
Of Girles and Boyes,
Of sweeter pledges send you,
And know no strife
'Twixt Man and Wife,
But all the Blessings send you.

[Exeunt.

[Enter **LADY FANCY**, and **SIR MERCURY POET**, coming out of the Bridal-Chamber together.

SIR MERCURY POET
Madam Fancy do not you wish to be a Bride, and that this night were your Wedding night?

LADY FANCY
I should be well content to be a Bride, and to have a Wedding day, conditionly the day would last to the end of my life; but mistake me not, I mean for the length of the day, not shortness of life.

SIR MERCURY POET
I perceive you would have no sleeping time.

LADY FANCY

You mistake, I would have no Wedding night.

[Exeunt.

[Enter **MONSIEUR FACIL** and **MONSIEUR ADVISER**.

MONSIEUR ADVISER

But are you seriously in love with the Lady Coy, the now Lady Amorous?

MONSIEUR FACIL

Yes seriously, but I may despair I shall never compass my desires.

MONSIEUR ADVISER

Faith, it is not probable you should obtain them, but yet you had best try.

MONSIEUR FACIL

That were but to plunge my self deeper into an unfortunate love.

MONSIEUR ADVISER

But a wise Man will omit no industry to compass his desires, neither do the Gods assist idle and cowardly Men.

MONSIEUR FACIL

But she is not only new Married, but so guarded with Modesty and Vertue, as unlawful love cannot get audience, much less a favour.

MONSIEUR ADVISER

Faith, if I were you, I would try in despite of her Modesty and Vertue.

MONSIEUR FACIL

I dare not.

MONSIEUR ADVISER

Fie! a Lover and a Coward! when the worst is but to be denied; but yet I would take many denials, before I would desist of my Suit; and if you do not pursue it, you partly deny your self.

MONSIEUR FACIL

How should I make my love known unto her?

MONSIEUR ADVISER

By some Lady confident, or she-servant Favourite; as also by Complemental Letters, and Love-Verses made in her praise; besides, making Balls and Collations to entertain her.

MONSIEUR FACIL
I'le take your Counsel.

[Enter **MIMICK** in hast.

MONSIEUR ADVISER
But stay, here comes Mimick the Lady Amorous Fool, who will be the fittest of all for this Employment; I'le speak to him: Stay, stay, honest friend, and let us speak a word or two.

[**MIMICK** goes on in hast.

MIMICK
God be with you, Sir.

MONSIEUR ADVISER
But will not you stay, a word or two?

MIMICK
Sir, I have stay'd twice two, that is four; nay by the Mass it was six at least; for you have asked me twice to stay, till you speak a word or two, and a word, and a word, and two and two is six, by my Calculation; and if you speak a word and two more, it will make three times three, that is just nine, the Golden Number, if I be not mistaken.

MONSIEUR ADVISER
You are right, friend.

MIMICK
A right friend is a great friend, and a great friend is a good friend; and so God be with you, Sir.

MONSIEUR ADVISER
Nay stay and tell me, are not you the Lady Amorous Mimick?

MIMICK
No truly, Sir, I am the Lady Vertue 's Mimick, and the Lady Amorous Fool.

MONSIEUR ADVISER
What, do you serve both the Ladies?

MIMICK
I am at both the Ladies service, Sir; God help me and give me Grace to please them well.

MONSIEUR ADVISER
Thou art an honest fellow.

MIMICK

But an honest fellow cannot serve two Mistresses, the more the pity!

MONSIEUR ADVISER
But you may serve this Gentleman, and he will serve thee; for if thou will but conveigh Letters, or can any way bring him to the private speech of the Lady Amorous, he will reward you bountifully.

MIMICK
I like the reward well; but I do not serve the Lady Amorous, but the Lady Vertue; but she being my Ladies Friend, and her Maid my Friend, I shall do my endeavour to deserve his gifts.

[Exit **MIMICK**.

MONSIEUR ADVISER
Faith, I doubt not, but our design will go on well.

MONSIEUR FACIL
I wish it may.

[Exit **MONSIEUR FACIL** at one door, and **MONSIEUR ADVISER** at another, who meets **MONSIEUR TAKE-PLEASURE** as in hast.

MONSIEUR ADVISER
Whether away so fast, Take-pleasure?

MONSIEUR TAKE-PLEASURE
I am going to a Company of Ladies that have sent for me.

MONSIEUR ADVISER
Let me go with you; for one Man can never please a company of Ladies; and surely it seems they are in great distress, otherwise they would not have sent for you in such hast.

MONSIEUR TAKE-PLEASURE
Not sent for me! why, what do you think of me?

MONSIEUR ADVISER
Why, I think you are a good fellow, and love a Mistress well; but I do not think you the Grand Signior.

MONSIEUR TAKE-PLEASURE
If I were, you should not come near my Seraglio.

MONSIEUR ADVISER
But let me go with thee to these Ladies, for they are not in a Seraglio, nor never will be; they love their liberty so well.

MONSIEUR TAKE-PLEASURE
I am content, upon condition, you do not so much as look upon those Ladies I court.

MONSIEUR ADVISER

But how if these Ladies look upon me?

MONSIEUR TAKE-PLEASURE
Yes, there is the mischief; therefore you shall not go.

MONSIEUR ADVISER
But if you let me go, I'le promise you, I'le wink to those Ladies that look on me.

MONSIEUR TAKE-PLEASURE
Winking is more dangerous then if you should plainly woo them; for winking is a kind of Wooing, and will win a Lady as soon as words will do.

MONSIEUR ADVISER
Then I will shut both my eyes.

MONSIEUR TAKE-PLEASURE
That will be worse, for that will put them in mind of going to bed; it will be like sleeping.

MONSIEUR ADVISER
Prithee let me go, and order me as you will.

MONSIEUR TAKE-PLEASURE
Wellcome, and as we go I'le tell you, how you shall behave your self to those Ladies.

MONSIEUR ADVISER
I will be govern'd according to your instructions.

[Exeunt.

SCENE II

[Enter **MADAM MEDIATOR**, and the **FEMALE-GUESTS**, the day after the Wedding, to the **LADY AMOROUS**, who sits in a shaded place, and Curtains drawn about her, a **MAID** stands by.

MADAM MEDIATOR
Where is the Lady Coy, the now Lady Amorous?

MAID
There; my Lady is within those Curtains.

MADAM MEDIATOR
Why are you so benighted, as to have your Curtains drawn so darkly about you?

LADY AMOROUS
I do not love the light.

MADAM MEDIATOR
Are you faln out with the light?

LADY AMOROUS
In truth I am ashamed to see the light.

MADAM MEDIATOR
Ashamed! let's see your face, whether you blush or not?

[The **LADY** offers to draw the Curtain, the **LADY AMOROUS** endeavours to hold it, and hideth her self behind it.

LADY AMOROUS
O fie! for Cupid and Venus sake do not look upon me, for if you do, I shall die with blushing.

LADIES
Come, come, we will see you.

LADY AMOROUS
I'le rather run away.

[She runs away, the **LADIES** follow her, and meet the **LADY VERTUE**.

MADAM MEDIATOR
Madam, we were a going to see how you appear, since you are a Wife.

LADY VERTUE
I hope I do not appear worse then I did, when I was a Maid; for I have not been Married so long as to have Children, Cares and Troubles, to decay my Youth and Beauty.

MADAM MEDIATOR
No, but we did imagine you would have been as most Brides are, shame-faced, and out of Countenance.

LADY VERTUE
Why so, since Marriage is lawful, honest, and honourable? for if Marriage had been an act, that deserves a blush, I would not have Married.

2ND LADY
But the Lady Coy, the now Lady Amorous, your fellow-Bride, is so out of Countenance, and doth so blush, as she is asham'd to appear in the light, and is forced to shut her eyes through shame, when her Husband looks upon her.

LADY VERTUE
Why, hath she deceived her Husband? was she not a Virgin when she Married, that she is so out of Countenance as not to return her Husbands looks.

2ND LADY
No, it is, that she is so extream modest.

LADY VERTUE
Modesty is only ashamed of dishonesty, and not of that, which is honest to the Laws of God, Nature, and all civil Nations and People; but to answer for my self, if my Husband approves, likes, and is pleased with me, I have no reason to be out of Countenance; and I hope my Vertue is such, as not to be ashamed of the light: But come Ladies, I have prepared a Banquet, to which I invite you, to join with me in rejoicing at my happy Union.

[Exeunt.

SCENE III

Enter **MONSIEUR ADVISER**, and **MONSIEUR FACIL**, to **MONSIEUR COURTLY,** who is sitting at the Table, and writing.

MONSIEUR ADVISER
What! writing!

MONSIEUR COURTLY
I am casting up some Accounts.

MONSIEUR ADVISER
Faith, I will see what a good Husband you are.

[He takes up the Paper.

MONSIEUR COURTLY
That Paper is the account of yesterday's expence.

MONSIEUR ADVISER
I can judge by a day's expence a week's, and by a week's a year's.

MONSIEUR COURTLY
That you cannot, for some days and weeks are more expensive then others.

MONSIEUR ADVISER
Faith, at the years end several sums comes to one and the same yearly sum, as so much yearly spent.

MONSIEUR COURTLY
Indeed for the most part it doth.

MONSIEUR ADVISER
Leave your talking, and let me read your Expences, this is the yesterday's expence; let me see, here is the account of the expence of Ushering four Ladies.
Imprimis, To a Sexton, to place four Ladies in several Pews in a Puritan Church, to hear a holy Brother preach, —2 Crowns.

Item, For Sillibubs in the Park for those Ladies,—20 s.

For two little baskets of Cherries, that hold some dozen Cherries a piece, but the first of this year, —15 s.

To the Keeper of the Park-gate,— half a Crown.

Item. for Cheesecakes and Rhennish-Wine in the fine Garden for those Ladies, — 20 s.

To a Fortune-teller, to tell those Ladies their Fortunes,—40 s.

Also to the Door-keeper of the Garden, half a Crown

Item. for a Supper for those Ladies at my Lodgings,—5 l.

To the Musick, — 3 l.

For Torches to light those Ladies home to their Lodgings,—5 shill.

The total comes to —13 l. 15 s.

You might have saved the 5 s. for Torch-light, by keeping those Ladies all night in your Lodgings.

MONSIEUR COURTLY

I should have been a loser by that thrift.

MONSIEUR FACIL

But do you spend every day thus much on Ladies?

MONSIEUR COURTLY

Not every day, but most days I do.

MONSIEUR ADVISER

And after one and the same manner, and in the same places, and with the same Ladies?

MONSIEUR COURTLY

No, I have variety for my money.

MONSIEUR FACIL

Why, that is some comfort to you, and pleasure to the Ladies; but will it hold out?

MONSIEUR COURTLY

No, faith, for neither my purse nor person will hold out; wherefore I must leave off to play the Gentleman-usher to Ladies, and go into the Country.

MONSIEUR ADVISER

You had better be the fore-horse in a Cart, then first Gentleman-usher in a Coach; ushering is so laborious; besides, the intollerable charge; in so much that you may with less expence maintain a whole Village of Country Wives with their Daughters and Maidservants, then entertain one Lady; moreover, those Villages will serve you, when as you are forced through civility to serve the Ladies.

MONSIEUR COURTLY

You say true; therefore I'le go into the Country.

MONSIEUR ADVISER

But will not those Ladies follow you?

MONSIEUR COURTLY

I cannot tell.

MONSIEUR ADVISER
Let me tell you, That is to be consider'd; and I would not have you go into the Country, for I and the rest of your friends would be sorry to lose your Company.

MONSIEUR COURTLY
Faith, the Ladies ingross me so much, as I have no time to say my Prayers, or to think of my self, much less to keep Company with my friends.

MONSIEUR FACIL
It seems you do not take the Ladies to be your friends.

MONSIEUR COURTLY
If they be, they are very troublesome, and chargeable friends, which Friends, I could be well content to be quit off, if I could tell how or which way.

MONSIEUR ADVISER
There be a hundred wayes to shake off those Ladies, if you will.

MONSIEUR COURTLY
No faith, I cannot; for they stick as close as burres, unless I should rudely quarrel with them, and basely raile against them; and if I did, it would be a question still whether I should be quit of them?

MONSIEUR ADVISER
Let me advise you, how you may civilly be quit of them.

MONSIEUR COURTLY
I shall gladly follow your advice.

MONSIEUR ADVISER
Do not visit them, out of some pretence you are not well.

MONSIEUR COURTLY
If I do not visit them, they'l visit me.

MONSIEUR ADVISER
Then pretend some Law-suit.

MONSIEUR COURTLY
Faith, they will follow me, and go to all the Courts of Judicature, to hear my Cause pleaded and judged.

MONSIEUR ADVISER
Then go to a Tavern every day, they will not follow you thither.

MONSIEUR COURTLY
Yes faith, some of them will, at least to the Tavern door in their Coaches to require my Company; but howsoever, they will send messenger after messenger to hasten me to them, pretending earnest business; and when I come, 'tis either to usher them to a Play, or to Church, or to the Exchange, or to

the places of pleasure, or to the Fields, Park, or Garden, or else to some Ball, or particular meeting, or to some Picture-drawer, or to play at Cards, or the like; and to Man them to these places, they will send to me, before I am up or awake; the truth is, they will not let me rest in quiet.

MONSIEUR FACIL
But this is a slavish life.

MONSIEUR COURTLY
It is so.

MONSIEUR ADVISER
But do they never reward thy service, Courtly?

MONSIEUR COURTLY
Yes, as the Devil doth his Servants.

MONSIEUR ADVISER
How is that?

MONSIEUR COURTLY
With fire; for they send me hot burning Spirits, which are called Cordials.

MONSIEUR ADVISER
It seems they think you want strength.

MONSIEUR COURTLY
I must needs, when they tire me off my legs, ushering them from place to place.

MONSIEUR FACIL
Do they give thee no Amorous favours?

MONSIEUR COURTLY
Yes; but they are better pleased, I should prevent them, and take favours from them before they are presented.

MONSIEUR FACIL
But that is some recompence for thy time and charge.

MONSIEUR COURTLY
The recompence, if you call it so, is the worse; for I had rather give them my Estate, then receive their Rewards; for though they make their favours, as a reward to their Courting-servants; yet their rewards are their chief pleasures, and the rewarded pains, for their Courting servants, lose more health by their favours, then they get wealth in their service.

MONSIEUR ADVISER
The last advice is, You must be as if you were drunk.

MONSIEUR COURTLY
That advice is worst of all; for then they are so busie, and make such puddering about me, to lay me to sleep, as they make me almost mad.

MONSIEUR ADVISER
You have said so much, as I perceive your own advice is the best, to go into the Country; and if the Country will not save your body, life and estate, from these Locust-Ladies, you must travel into some other Kingdom.

MONSIEUR COURTLY
If I do, they will follow me; for Ladies are as far-travellers in this age, as the Men; and I know some Gentlemen that are followed by Ladies out of one Kingdom into another, so as they do not know whether to go, for the World is not sufficient to hide or obscure them from the Ladies search.

MONSIEUR ADVISER
Why, then most of the Men must turn Fryers, for that is to live in this world, as if they liv'd out of it.

MONSIEUR COURTLY
That shift will not serve their turn; for if the Cavaliers turn Fryers, the Ladies will turn Nunnes, and then make those Fryers their Confessors.

MONSIEUR ADVISER
Then there is no way for Men to escape those Ladies followers.

MONSIEUR COURTLY
Yes, there is one way.

MONSIEUR ADVISER
What way is that?

MONSIEUR COURTLY
You must excuse me, for I will not declare it.

[Exeunt.

[Enter **MONSIEUR FACIL**, and he speaks to himself.

MONSIEUR FACIL
I wonder Mimick stays so long, and doth not bring me an answer yet, from the Lady Amorous.

[Enter **MIMICK**.

But here he is.

MONSIEUR FACIL
Monsieur Mimick! well met; have you delivered my Letter to the Lady Amorous?

MIMICK
Yes, Mr. Facil, I did deliver it to her.

MONSIEUR FACIL
And how did she receive it?

MIMICK
Faith, she received your Letter, as all Women do Love-Presents.

MONSIEUR FACIL
How is that?

MIMICK
With an outward dislike, and an inward affection.

MONSIEUR FACIL
If she received my Letter, with a displeased countenance, I judg she doth not love me.

MIMICK
Then your judgment is not wise; for love lives not in the countenance, but in the heart.

MONSIEUR FACIL
But the Countenance expresses love; for a well pleased Countenance, expresses a well affected heart.

MIMICK
If you ground your belief on a Womans Countenance, you will be deceived; for Womens Countenances for the most part are as false as their faces; the one is glast with smiles, as the other with Pomatum; and dissembling modesty is like Spanish Red, which is soon rub'd off with acquaintance and jealousie; or a peevish humour wipes off their smiles; so that there is no trust in their Countenances; for they change every minute of an hour; wherefore, they are unskilful Men, and unhappy Lovers, that steer the course of their desires, by the Card of their Mistresses Countenances, which vary almost every moment, or by the Stars of their Mistresses eyes, which are wandring Planets. The truth is, most Lovers have troublesome Voyages in love, by reason all Womens minds are as inconstant as the wind.

MONSIEUR FACIL
But I hope, by your favour and industry for me, to the Lady, my Voyage will be easie and free.

MIMICK
Do you believe I have power on your Mistress mind, as the Witches of Lapland have on the Winds?

MONSIEUR FACIL
Faith, Monkies, Dogs, Parrots, and Fools, are powerful with Women, especially with Ladies.

MIMICK
Then deliver your Love-Letters to the
Ladies Monkys, tell your Love-Messages to the Ladies
Parrots, and give your Love-Collations to the Ladies
Dogs, and your Love-bribes to my Ladies Fool.

MONSIEUR FACIL
It is the easiest way; only to employ her Fool, and to encourage you, I give you five Pounds for the present, and more I promise you hereafter, to plead my suit, and to speak in my behalf.

MIMICK
Faith, your case is so bad, as it requires a witty and ingenuous knave to make it seem a good case, and an eloquent Orator to make it seem a clear case; for Oratory makes a foul case seem fair, and great fees makes an Orator's wit quick, and his tongue smooth.

MONSIEUR FACIL
Well, I will trust to your Knavery, wish well to your Oratory, and hope Fortune will favour your Wisdom.

MIMICK
You mistake; for Fortune never favours wise Men, but Fools.

[Exit **MONSIEUR FACIL**.

MIMICK
Well, craft shall serve for wisdom, and the chief part of my craft must be to Fool this Lover, or rather to cozen him; for Lovers are Fools of Cupid 's making, and they wear Fools Coats in Cupid 's Court.

[Exeunt.

[Enter the **LADY VERTUE**, and **SIR WILLIAM SAGE**. **MIMICK**, who seems to be in a very serious study, not taking any notice of his **MASTER** and **LADY**.

SIR WILLIAM SAGE
Surely Mimick has State-matters in his head, he is so studious and serious.

LADY VERTUE
Mimick?

[He doth not answer.

LADY VERTUE
Why Mimick, are you deaf?

MIMICK
I am somewhat thick of hearing.

SIR WILLIAM SAGE
But Mimick, let us know what is the cause you are in so serious a study.

MIMICK
I am considering with my self, what profession I shall be of.

LADY VERTUE

And what Profession have you chosen to be of?

MIMICK
I have not chosen any as yet, for I waver in my mind amongst many Professions, as an amorous Lover doth amongst many Ladies, not resolving which to address himself to; for though he would enjoy them all, yet he can court but one at a time; and though he resolveth to court all, yet he can but enjoy one at a time.

SIR WILLIAM SAGE
But he may court and enjoy them all, one after another.

MIMICK
Faith, that is an endless work; for before the last Lady is courted and enjoyed, he will be forced to be of the Profession of a Priest, to preach his own funeral Sermon, or of a Sexton, to dig his own grave: But leaving Priests and amorous Lovers, what Profession shall I be of?

LADY VERTUE
What think you of being a Courtier?

MIMICK
There are so many Court-fools, that they never thrive with that Profession; for what they get by flattery, they spend in vanity.

LADY VERTUE
What think you of being a Lawyer?

MIMICK
The Law is more of the Knaves then the Fool's side, therefore I shall never thrive in that Profession.

SIR WILLIAM SAGE
What think you of being a Merchant?

MIMICK
I could Traffick with Jest, but I am afraid in some of my Ventures I should have my head broke; therefore, I will not be of that Profession.

LADY VERTUE
What think you of being a States-man?

MIMICK
Faith, I think I am fool enough to be a States-man, but I have not Formality enough; besides, I shall make such disorders and disturbances in State-affairs, as I may chance to be kill'd in an uproar or seditious Tumult.

SIR WILLIAM SAGE
What think you of being a Soldier?

MIMICK

No, for I am more safe from danger in my Fools Coat, then they in their Iron-arms; and shall get more by a Fool's Profession, then a Soldiers.

SIR WILLIAM SAGE

What think you of being a Scholar?

MIMICK

That I am now; for I learn every day to play the Fool better and better.

LADY VERTUE

What think you of being a City-Magistrate?

MIMICK

I like that the best; for my Fools Coat will serve for my Magistrates Gown; but yet I am afraid of the Common-people in these seditious times.

SIR WILLIAM SAGE

What think you of being a Traveller?

MIMICK

O Lord! so I may travel to my wit's end.

LADY VERTUE

What think you of being a Chymist?

MIMICK

Faith, I get more Gold by playing the Fool with Lords and Ladies, then Chymists do by playing the Fools with Fire and Furnace.

SIR WILLIAM SAGE

Then I think you had best continue your own Profession still, which is to play the Fool.

MIMICK

But my Profession of playing the Fool is a general Profession, and I would fain have a particular Profession; for there are few Men but have some other Profession besides their Natural Profession; Wherefore, I must study some other Profession.

LADY VERTUE

What do you think then of being a Vintner?

MIMICK

My Guests will drink up my Wine, and leave me their Scores; lie with my Wife, and give her the Pox; and if I have not a handsom Woman to my Wife, I shall have no Guests.

LADY VERTUE

What think you of being a Taylor?

MIMICK

I shall have only my Measures for my pains, and the shreds for my labour.

SIR WILLIAM SAGE
What think you of being a Usurer?

MIMICK
So a Fool and his Money would be soon parted, and I shall have bonds for my Money; but a hundred to one if I get my Money by the bonds.

LADY VERTUE
What think you of being an Amorous Lover?

MIMICK
I shall woo more Mistresses, then I shall win, and win more Mistresses then I shall use.

LADY VERTUE
But you may get a rich Wife, if you Woo well.

MIMICK
If I should woo the best of any Man, I shall sooner get the Pox with a Mistress, then Wealth with a Wife; for Fortune is the only Match-maker.

SIR WILLIAM SAGE
But there is a saying, That Fools have Fortune.

MIMICK
Not all fools; for there be more Fools then good fortune; the truth is, There are so many Fools, as it is impossible for Fortune to favour them all.

LADY VERTUE
But Fortune may favour those that are most foolish.

MIMICK
Then she will not favour me; wherefore I'le reject Fortune, relie upon my own wit.

LADY VERTUE
Your Wit is so weak, as it cannot uphold you.

MIMICK
I'le try the strength of it, and when I fall for want of Wit, it is a proper time for Fortune to raise me up to shew her power.

SIR WILLIAM SAGE
Well, we will leave you to your study, and when you have chosen a Profession, I suppose you will make us acquainted with it.

MIMICK
No doubt of it; for yon must help to put me into practise.

[Exeunt.

[Enter **MR LONG-LIFE**, and **MR AGED**.

MR AGED
Longlife. How are you since you went abroad?

MR LONG-LIFE
Very well, I thank you Mr. Aged.

MR AGED
I am now come to you, to ask you a question, whether you would not think it were wise for us, we having only two Children you, a Son and I a Daughter, to match them together, and so we being both rich, we may joyn our Estates together, by joyning our Children together which will make them both flow in plenty,

MR LONG-LIFE
I like your proposition, concerning the joyning our riches together, by joyning our Children together: But my Son is a Wit, Mr. Aged, and your Daughter I hear is a Wit; and if their wits be joyned together, it may over power their Wealth; for Wit and Wealth doth never agree together; For wit regards not Wealth, and wealth regards not wit; which is the reason that those, which have most Wit, (which are Poets) are poor; For you shall seldom read, or hear, That natutal Poets are rich. And both our Children being Poetical, should we marry them together, would undo them.

MR AGED
By the Mass, you say true.

MR LONG-LIFE
Then we must endeavour to marry our Children to Fooles; you must provide a foolish man for your Daughter, and I a foolish woman for my Son; That the dulness of the Fool, may allay the quickness of the Wit, which will make a good temper, causing them to thrive in wealth, and to increase Posterity; for let me tell you, That great Wits for the most part have few Children, but what their brain produces, which are Ideas, Inventions and Opinions; Ideas are Daughters; Inventions are Sons, and Opinions ermaphrodites; and the production of these Incorporeal Children, hinders the production of Corporeal Children; and we both desire to have Corporeal Grand-Children to uphold our Families.

MR AGED
You say wisely, Mr. Long-life; and therefore, we must endeavour to marry our Children to Fools, for the Wealth and Posterities of our Families.

[Exeunt.

ACT III

SCENE I

[Enter **SIR JOHN AMOROUS**, and his **LADY**.

LADY

Sir John, Sir John, I take it very unkindly, that you should go abroad, and leave my Company?

SIR JOHN AMOROUS

Sometimes, Wife, to be absent from each other, is a refreshment, and Temperance is part of Prudence.

LADY

I love not such Refreshments, Temperance, and Prudence; wherefore, you must either stay at home and keep me Company, or I shall seek other Company elsewhere.

[Exit **LADY**. **SIR JOHN AMOROUS** Solus.

SIR JOHN AMOROUS

That will be some ease; for I had rather be a Cuckold then be bound to one Woman, especially my Wife.

[Enter his Wife's **MAID**.

SIR JOHN AMOROUS

Mal, I'le prefer thee.

MAID

I thank you, Master.

SIR JOHN AMOROUS

I'le prefer thee from my Servant, to be my Mistress.

MAID

If you had been unmarried, and would prefer me from being your Mistress, to be your Wife, I should have taken it for an honour.

SIR JOHN AMOROUS

But I am Married, Mal, and thou shalt take thy Ladie's place, in thy Ladie's absence.

MAID

I had rather Marry Tom your Butler lawfully, then lie with my Master unlawfully.

SIR JOHN AMOROUS

Why, Mal, Love is lawful, and to serve your Master is lawful; wherefore, it is lawful to serve your Master's Love.

MAID

But some kinds of Love are unlawful, and some kinds of Service are unlawful; for it is unlawful to love Vice, and unlawful to serve the Devil; wherefore it is unlawful to be my Master's Whore.

SIR JOHN AMOROUS

To be your Master's Whore, is to be your Master's Mistress; and to be the Butler's Wife, is to be the Butler's Slave; but I'le leave you to the Butler's droppings of his Taps: But howsoever, Consider it well, Mal, for you will be good enough for the Butler afterwards.

[Exeunt.

SCENE II

Enter **SIR WILLIAM SAGE** and his **LADY**.

SIR WILLIAM SAGE
I wonder that Mimick is not here! for his Company is very delightful, to pass away idle; time for idle time is only free for Fools Company.

LADY
He is rather a Knave then a Fool; but here he comes.

[Enter **MIMICK**.

SIR WILLIAM SAGE
Mimick, have you chosen a Profession yet?

MIMICK
Yes, marry have I, for I intend to be an Orator.

SIR WILLIAM SAGE
If you be a professed Orator, I suppose you have studied a speech.

MIMICK
Yes, I have studied, as Orators use to do, in making an Oration; for I have rackt my Brain, stretch'd my Wit, strapado'd my Memory, tortured my thoughts, and kept my Sences awake.

SIR WILLIAM SAGE
Certainly, it is a very eloquent and wise Oration, since you have taken so much pains.

MIMICK
Labour and Study is not a certain rule for wise, witty, or eloquent Orations or Speeches; for many studied Speeches are very foolish: But will you hear my Speech?

SIR WILLIAM SAGE
I will.

MIMICK
But then Master, you must stand for, signifie, or represent a Multitude, or an Assembly.

SIR WILLIAM SAGE

That is impossible, being but a single person.

MIMICK

Why doth not a single Figure stand for a Number, as the Figure of Five, Eight or Nine, and joining Ciphers to them, they stand for so many Hundreds, or Thousands: And here be two Joint-Stools, one of which Stools and you Lady shall serve for two Ciphers and my Master for the Figure of Nine, and so you two and the Joint-Stool make Nine hundred.

SIR WILLIAM SAGE

But if the Assembly be so big, as to be a Company of Nine hundred they cannot all stand so near, as to hear what you speak, neither ean your voice reach to the Circumferent Ears.

MIMICK

The greatest Glory of an Orator is to have Crouds of People follow him, and those that hear the least will praise him the most; and the truth is, That all Orators gain more renown by those that do not hear them, but only see them, then by those that stand so near, as to hear what they speak; for there is ten to one of those that do not hear them, to those that do hear chem; So that if those that do hear them, should dispraise their Orations, yet those that hear them not, will commend them, and having ten to one of their side, they may say what they will, they shall be applauded, and the most Voices carry them up to Fame's Tower; which considering, I will set another Joint-stool as another Cipher to my Lady, and three Ciphers, with the Figure of Nine, my Master, will make it Nine thousand.

SIR WILLIAM SAGE

As many as you please.

MIMICK

But what shall I have for a Pulpit or standing place? for I must mount above all the Assembly?

LADY

Take another Joint-stool, and stand upon that.

MIMICK

O fie! that will not appear well; besides, I shall stand tottering, ready to fall, and the very fear of falling, will put me out of my Speech.

LADY

But you will appear standing upon a Joint-stool, like as a Statue upon a Pedistal.

MIMICK

I should be well pleased to have a Statue made for me, and set up as an honour and remembrance of me; but I shall not be pleased to stand as a Statue my self.

SIR WILLIAM SAGE

Why then get a Tub; and stand in that.

MIMICK

A Tub will not do me any service, unless it be a mounted Tub. But for this time I'le stand upon the Table, without Tub or Case, to speak the naked truth; and thus I ascend.

[He ascends upon the Table.

LADY
Begin.

MIMICK
Stay, I must breathe first, hawk, spit, blow my nose, humm, and look gravely round about upon the People, and then speak at first in a low voice, then raise my Voice by degrees, until I come to the highest strain or point.

[He Speaks.

NOBLE, Honourable, and Worthy Auditors, I am come here to speak of a Subject which concerns all Men; which General Subject is Women; and I am not only to Treat of Women, which is an easie Subject to be Treated of; but of the Chastity of Women, which is an hard, frozen Subject; and so hard frozen it is, that all the heat Love can bring is not able to thaw it; the truth is, Chastity is a Subject, that lives at a great distance; for though the two Names, Woman and Chastity, are oft-times joined together, yet the several Subjects of those Names, dwell not near each other; for Chastity dwells at the Poles, where no Woman is; and Women dwell or inhabit the Torrid Zone, where no Chastity is: Thus you may perceive that Names are more easily joined, then the things they signifie; but how to bring Chastity and Women together, is the difficulty, indeed so difficult as it is impossible; and as impossible as for hot Hell and cold Heaven to meet, or for gods and devils to be friends: But noble Auditors the Names Chast Women being join'd together, are sufficient; for that Conjunction of Names contents, satisfies and pleases all Men, as Fathers, Sons, Brothers and Husbands, that would have their Daughters, Sisters, Mothers and Wives Chast; and as for Amorous Lovers, they are pleased to have the Subjects dwell at distance; so that Art and Nature, Deceit and Verity have agreed together to make all Men happy, so far as concerns Women.

LADY
Leave off your Prating, or I'le fling one of these Ciphers at your head.

MIMICK
Will not you let me speak out my Oration?

LADY
No, unless it were better.

MIMICK
If you will let me speak out my Speech, I'le make the two Poles meet in the very forehead of the Torrid Zone of a Man's head.

LADY
I'le hear no more; wherefore, come off from the Table.

MIMICK
Well, I obey, although I am vexed at the heart, that I must not speak out my Speech, as also to be disgraced before an Assembly of Nine thousand.

LADY

You knavish Fool, what cause invited, perswaded, or commanded you to speak an Oration concerning the Chastity of Women?

MIMICK

That which perswaded me to speak an Oration, and not only an Oration, but a factious or malicious Oration was that which perswaded all Orators; first, felf-love to shew their Wit; next, their ill Nature to make a division and dissention amongst Mankind.

LADY

Well, since you have express'd the evil Orators of these evil times, such as make Factions and Divisions; I will express such Orators as ought to be; and thus I'le speak to this Assembly.

[She Speaks.

NOBLE, Honourable and Worthy Auditors, I am come here to contradict a Knavish Fool, that has spoken to the Disgrace of Women; saying, That only the Names of Women and Chastity are joined together, but the Subjects dwell far asunder; which is false; for though some Women, as the scum of the Female Sex, be Incontinent, yet all Women are not so; for some Women are Chast by Nature, others by Vertue, and some by Honour: As for Vertue and Honour, they are like to Plants set or planted by Education, and grow up like to tall Cedars or strong Oaks in the Mind, which bear no evil fruits; as Vices and base qualities, or evil and dishonest desires: But Worthy Auditors, give me leave to tell you, That Women are the unhappiest Creatures which Nature ever made; not only that they are the most shiftless Creatures, but the most abused of any other Creatures, and only by Men; who do not only continually assault them, and endeavour to corrupt and betray them, but they have enslaved them, and do often defame them with slanders and reproaches, vain glorious boasts, and lying brags; the truth is, Men are like Devils to Women, seeking whom they may devour; inticing, alluring, perswading and flattering Women, to the ruine of their Souls, Bodies, Minds, Fortunes, and good Names; but Women are beloved and favoured by the gods, who endue their Bodies with Beauty, and their Minds with Spiritual Grace, their Thoughts with Religious Zeal, and their Lives with Pious Devotions; which keeps their Bodies Chast, their Minds pure, and their Lives Vertuous: But those few Women that are Incontinent, are rather Beasts then Women; but most Women are Angelical; and though Men defame them, yet the Gods glorifie them.

MIMICK

Lady, if you speak any longer of the Female Subject, you will cast them from Heaven into Hell; for you cannot go beyond Heaven, Angels and Gods.

LADY

I am content to speak no more of them at this time, but leave them in bliss.

SIR WILLIAM SAGE

Mimick, your Lady will be too hard for you.

MIMICK

Yes in Foolery, but not in Wit.

[Exeunt.

SCENE III

[Enter **MONSIEUR ADVISER**, and **MONSIEUR COURTLY**.

MONSIEUR COURTLY
WHERE were you, that I did not see you all yesterday, nor most part of this day?

MONSIEUR ADVISER
Faith, I was all the Morning at a Sermon, and at Noon I went to a Tavern, in the Afternoon I went to a Play, and at night I went to a Common-house, and from thence I went to the Gaming-house, and there I stay'd till late in the Morning; and then I went home, and lay and slept so long, as I have but newly dined.

MONSIEUR COURTLY
Dined, say you! why it is almost Supper-time.

MONSIEUR ADVISER
Not with me.

MONSIEUR COURTLY
No; for you turn the Day into Night, and Night into Day.

MONSIEUR ADVISER
I did not so yesterday.

MONSIEUR COURTLY
Yes, but you did; for you spent all the day in deeds of darkness.

MONSIEUR ADVISER
Will you say, that hearing a Sermon is a deed of darkness?

MONSIEUR COURTLY
Yes, unless you did profit by it, which I do not perceive you did; the truth is, by your after-actions you seem the worse for it.

MONSIEUR ADVISER
I'le confess to you, my friend, that the Sermon made me so dull and melancholy, as I was forced to go to a Tavern, to revive and comfort my Mind with some Spiritual Liquor; and from thence I went to a Play to recreate my Thoughts, and to take them from all sad Contemplations, in seeing and hearing a merry Comedy acted; and the truth is, the Play made me so lively, as I became so wanton, that I was forced to go to a Common-house, and after I had convers'd with the Woman, I was as dull and melancholy as I was after the Sermon; so then I went to the Gaming-house for diversion, knowing I should meet store of Company; and being there, I fell to play, where I lost all my Money; for which I was so troubled, as I wish my self dead, having not any Money left to live; and being moneyless, I went home to bed, that I might sleep and forget my loss for a time.

MONSIEUR COURTLY
But did not the thoughts of the loss hinder your sleep?

MONSIEUR ADVISER
No faith; for my thoughts were so opprest with grief, as they fell fast asleep, and so fast asleep they were, as I did not dream.

MONSIEUR COURTLY
But now they are awake, they remember your losses, do they not?

MONSIEUR ADVISER
Yes, but I will perswade you to go with me to the
Tavern, there to drink out the remembrance.
For when my head is fill'd with Vaporous Wine,
My thoughts for Losses will not then repine.

[Enter **MONSIEUR TAKE-PLEASURE** to **MONSIEUR ADVISER** and **MONSIEUR COURTLY**.

MONSIEUR COURTLY
Tom, Thou art welcome.

MONSIEUR TAKE-PLEASURE
Go hang your self, for you are not a Man of your word, for you promis'd to meet me at the Crown-Tavern, where I stay'd for you till twelve a Clock last night, expecting your coming.

MONSIEUR COURTLY
And how did you pass away the solitary time?

MONSIEUR TAKE-PLEASURE
Faith, I call'd for some Tobacco, and a pint of Wine, and then I took a Pipe, then drunk a glass of Wine, and you did not come; then I took another Pipe, and drunk another glass of Wine, and you did not come; so I took Pipe after Pipe, and drunk Glass after Glass, until the Pint-pot was empty; then I call'd for another Pint, and another Pint, and drunk them as the first; and still you stay'd, and still I drunk so long as I was almost drunk, expecting your Company; but at last finding my Stomack full, and my head light, and the night far spent I went home and so to bed.

MONSIEUR ADVISER
Without saying your Prayers?

MONSIEUR TAKE-PLEASURE
Faith, I could not say my Prayers for Cursing of Courtly; but at last I sell asleep with a Curse in my mouth, which Curse I found in my mouth when I did awake in the morning.

MONSIEUR ADVISER
Did you swallow the Curse down, or spit it out?

MONSIEUR TAKE-PLEASURE

Faith, it had almost choak'd me; for it stuck so in my Throat, as I could neither get it up, nor down, but at last I spit it out, for it was as bitter as Gall.

MONSIEUR COURTLY
You had no reason to curse me, if you were drunk; for the only design of our meeting at the Tavern, was but to be drunk.

MONSIEUR TAKE-PLEASURE
That is true; but there is no pleasure to be drunk without a Companion.

MONSIEUR COURTLY
The truth is, I could not come; for I was forced against my will to Sup with a Lady.

MONSIEUR TAKE-PLEASURE
Faith, Women spoile all good fellowship; but I had been better Company for her last night, then you were.

MONSIEUR COURTLY
Come, come, let us go to the same Tavern, and there end all Quarrels.

[Exeunt.

SCENE IV

[Enter **MONSIEUR FACIL**, and **MIMICK**.

MONSIEUR FACIL
Master Mimick, I am come according to your appointment.

MIMICK
Then Mr. Facil you may depart according to my appointment.

MONSIEUR FACIL
But you assured me, That if I came at this hour, I should have access to your Lady.

MIMICK
But Women change their mind every minute, and are in threescore several minds or humors in an hour; and this minute the Lady is in a very angry humor, which will not agree with your amorous humor.

MONSIEUR FACIL
But I'le stay until her angry humor is past.

MIMICK
Then you may stay until you be weary; for she will change out of one angry humor into another, until she hath run out an hour; for there be many several kinds and sorts of angry Humors.

MONSIEUR FACIL
But I will stay an hour.

MIMICK
But if you do, it is not likely that the Lady will be in a humor to entertain your Courtly address; for it is probable, as being most usual, that from the last angry humor, she will change into the first degree of a Melancholy humor.

MONSIEUR FACIL
Then I will attend two hours, until such time as she will be out of her Melancholy humor.

MIMICK
That will not do you any service; for out of the last Melancholy humor she will change into a pious humor, and so from one pious humor into another, until such time as she comes to weep like a Mary Magdalen, and after floods of Tears she will fall fast asleep; her Sences and Spirits being tired with Kneeling, Praying, Sighing and Weeping, and after she awakes from her devout sleep, she may chance to bestow a Charity upon you.

MONSIEUR FACIL
I'le attend in hope of that Charity.

MIMICK
I perceive by you, that Lovers will take no excuses or denials; but yet this last I hope will drive you away, which is, The Lady has the Wind-collock; wherefore she will not admit of a visit, especially Amorous Suiters this day.

MONSIEUR FACIL
By this I find that you have fill'd me with hope, to delude me.

MIMICK
Let me tell you, that Love is the greatest Deluder, or Cheater, especially Amorous Love; but to keep you from dispair, I'le promise you (for Promises keep Lovers alive) I will devise some way to corrupt this Lady to your desires, although it requires much labour, study, wit, and time, to corrupt Chastity; and since my Service will be great, my Reward must not be small.

MONSIEUR FACIL
Then here I give you Ten pounds to reward your Knavery.

[Exit **MONSIEUR FACIL**, **MIMICK** Solus.

MIMICK
Why, this is right as it should be, for one
Knave to Fee another, that Knavery may thrive.

[Exeunt.

[Enter **SIR MERCURY POET**, and the **LADY FANCY**.

SIR MERCURY POET
Madam, I take it for a great favour and obligation, that you will receive my visit.

LADY FANCY
It would be an Obligation to my self, to oblige a worthy person, such as I believe you are, but I do not perceive how I can merit thanks in receiving your Visit, for I suppose you can better pass your time, then with my dull Company, and unprofitable Conversation.

SIR MERCURY POET
It is a particular favour, because you do not not usually receive Visits.

LADY FANCY
The reason why I do not usually receive Visits, is out of a respect to the Visiters, knowing I have not Wit to entertain them, Speech to delight them, nor Learning to profit them; so they would but lose their time in visiting me; and I chuse rather to lofe the profit I might gain by hearing wise, witty, and learned Visiters; then they should lose their time by learning nothing themselves; for Wisdom and Wit desires to advance in Knowledg, and not to stand at a stay; for though prating Fools take pleasure to inform, and formal Fools to reform; yet wise Men delight to be informed and reformed, through a noble ambition to attain to perfecton.

SIR MERCURY POET
Which Perfection, Madam, you have arrived to.

LADY FANCY
That is impossible, for Nature hath made Women so defective, as they are not capable of Perfection.

SIR MERCURY POET
Madam, my Soul is wedded to your Vertue, and my Contemplations to your Fancy, and my
Love and Person longs to be wedded to your
Beauty and Chastity.
And if our Wits agree,
I'm sure you'l favour me.
For Wit the Brain doth move,
And causes Souls to love:
For Fools cannot love well,
Nor reason for Love tell;
They understand not Merit,
Nor a Coelestial Spirit.

[Enter **MR AGED**.

MR AGED
How is that! Merit, Spirit, and I know not what! Daughter, I am come to forbid you the Company of Sir Mercury Poet, and that you receive not any of his Visits: And Sir Mercury Poet, I do forbid you my Daughters Company.

SIR MERCURY POET

Sir, I have not visited your Daughter, without your leave; for you were pleased to invite me to wait on your Daughter.

MR AGED
'Tis true, for I did believe, (by reason your Father and I being old acquaintance, and loving friends, and both being rich, and having Children, he a Son, and I a Daughter) it might be very proper and fit to have agreed to have matched you together; but since your Father and I having debated and considered well upon the Case, we find it no ways profitable for either.

SIR MERCURY POET
Where is the disadvantage or hinderance?

MR AGED
Your Wit.

SIR MERCURY POET
Is Wit a Crime?

MR AGED
It ought to be made Criminal; for it is not only unprofitable, but ruinous; not any person thrives that has it; and it makes those that are rich, poor; and those that are poor, uncapable to be rich.

SIR MERCURY POET
They that have Wit, need no other wealth, Sir.

[Enter **MR LONG-LIFE**.

MR AGED
Mr. Longlife, I find now your words true,
That Wit regards not Wealth; for your Son says,
That Wit is Wealth enough of it self.

MR LONG-LIFE
Yes, yes, Mr. Aged; but he will find, Wit cannot buy Land, unless he joins Knavery to it.

SIR MERCURY POET
True Wit is always just, and honest, it knows no double dealing; and honour is the ground on which it builds a Fame.

MR LONG-LIFE
But if you have no other ground, nor other building, but Honour and Fame, you may beg for your livelihood, or starve for want of bread.

SIR MERCURY POET
I had rather die for want of bread, then live without honourable Fame; and Fortune's goods are poor to those that Nature gives.

MR LONG-LIFE

O Mr. Aged, I am unhappy, undone; for I perceive my Posterity will be all Beggars: And therefore, if you will not change your Principles soon, I will disinherit you.

SIR MERCURY POET
You cannot, Sir; for though you may give away your Land, you cannot give away my Wit (if I have any.)

MR LONG-LIFE
If I cannot, I will marry you to a Fool; so that though you be poor, your Children may be rich.

SIR MERCURY POET
If you please, Sir, and Mr. Aged consent, I desire I may Marry this Lady.

MR LONG-LIFE
No, no, Son she hath Wit, I know by her silence, otherwise her tongue would have run a race in this time.

LADY FANCY
I can speak Sir, but I doubt I have not Wit to speak well.

MR LONG-LIFE
Nay, if you talk of Wit, you are not for my Son.

LADY FANCY
Your Son hath so much Wit, that what Woman soever he Marries, cannot continue a Fool long, for she will get Wit from him, and yet he will have no less, for Nature still supplies his store.

MR LONG-LIFE
But my Grand-Children may be Fools, if my Son's Wife be none of Natures witty Daughters.

LADY FANCY
His Children cannot be Fools; for Wit begets Wit, although a Fool should be the breeder.

MR LONG-LIFE
Good Mr. Aged, lock up your Daughter, until I have sent my Son to Travel; for otherwise we shall ruin our Posterities.

[Exeunt.

ACT IV

SCENE I

[Enter **LADY AMOROUS, LADY VERTUE**, and **MADAM MEDIATOR**.

LADY AMOROUS

Madam, what makes you so fine to day? and not only your person is finer, but your house is finer trim'd and trickt, then usually it was; have you a Servant to visit you to day?

LADY VERTUE
No, but I have a Master that is to come out of the Country to day.

LADY AMOROUS
Who is your Master?

LADY VERTUE
My Husband, who comes home to day.

LADY AMOROUS
Do you make your self and your house so fine only for your Husband?

LADY VERTUE
Only for my Husband, say you! Why, he is the only Man that I desire to appear fine to; and the only person I desire to please and delight.

MADAM MEDIATOR
But Husbands take no notice of the bravery of their Wives.

LADY VERTUE
Howsoever, it is the part of every good wife to express, on all occasions, their Love and Respect to their Husbands; in their absence to mourn, at their return to rejoice, and in their Company to be best pleased.

MADAM MEDIATOR
Love, Respect and Duty, are only expressible in Humors, Words and Service, and not in Habit.

LADY VERTUE
But Joy is exprest in habit, as much as mourning; witness Triumphs and Triumphant Shews; and Triumphs of Joy, and Funerals, are not alike.

MADAM MEDIATOR
All Noble Persons are buried in Triumphs.

LADY VERTUE
Indeed they are buried with Ceremony, but it is such Ceremony as expresses Dolor, not Joy; for they are followed with black Mourners, and weeping eyes: But however, I endeavour to appear to my Husband, at his returning home, like a gay and joyful Bride, and not as a sad mourning Widow.

LADY AMOROUS
Let me not live, Lady Vertue, if you be not the most simple Woman alive.

LADY VERTUE
In what?

LADY AMOROUS

First,
That you can take pleasure in the dull Company of a Husband; next,
That you do not delight your self with the Gallants of the Times; and thirdly,
That you do not only spoile your own Husband, but all other Womens Husbands, with your example; for which folly, you ought to be condemned by all our Sex.

LADY VERTUE
If they condemn me for my Vertue, I will despise them for their Vices.

LADY AMOROUS
But Vice is a Vertue in this age; ask Madam Mediator else.

LADY VERTUE
What say you, Madam Mediator?

MADAM MEDIATOR
I say, that Vice was never so confident as it is now, nor never so glorified as it is now, nor never so beloved as it is now, nor never so practised as it is now.

LADY AMOROUS
Well, since Vice is so beloved, and Vertue despised, I will go to a merry Meeting. Come, Madam Mediator, you'l make one, although Lady Vertue will not.

[Exeunt.

SCENE II

[Enter **MONSIEUR FACIL**, and **MIMICK**.

MIMICK
Monsieur Facil, I have tired my Legs, and worn out the Soles of my Shooes to find you out, to give you a Letter from the Lady Amorous.

MONSIEUR FACIL
I am sorry you have taken such pains.

MIMICK
You may requite my pains when you please; but here is the Letter.

[He receives the Letter.

MONSIEUR FACIL
Faithful Mimick! happy Facil! divine Lady! delicious Letter!

[He kisses the Letter.

MIMICK
What delicious pleasure do you receive in that Kiss, Monsieur Facil?

MONSIEUR FACIL
As much pleasure as Joy can give me.

[He opens the Letter.

What is this, a plain sheet of Paper! you Rogue, do you abuse and cozen me?

MIMICK
Did not you give me Ten pound to reward my Knavery? for which I should be ungrateful, should I not be a Knave to you; but yet you have no reason to be angry for this unletter'd Paper, which is the royall'st Kindness, and most generous Present, the Lady could send you; for she has sent you a blank to write down your own desires, demands, or condition of agreement, love and friendship.

MONSIEUR FACIL
If it be so, I ask you Pardon, and will requite your fidelity with Gold.

MIMICK
I'le take your requital.

MONSIEUR FACIL
Pray go with me to my Lodgings, and there I'le write in this white Paper, that came from the whiter hands of my Mistress, my love and affections, and you shall guide it unto her.

MIMICK
You must ballace the Letter with Gold, or otherwise it will be drown'd in the returning-Voyage.

MONSIEUR FACIL
I will.

[Exeunt.

SCENE III

[Enter **LADY AMOROUS**, and **TWO** or **THREE** other **LADIES**.

1ST LADY
Lady Amorous, Marriage has made you a boon Companion.

LADY AMOROUS
I was a Novice before I married; but now I find that there is no pleasure, like Liberty, Mirth and good Company.

1ST LADY

You say true, Lady, for a Stoical life is the worst life in the World.

2ND LADY
But the Lady Vertue, and Sir W. Sage live the life of Stoicks.

LADY AMOROUS
The more Fools they; but my Husband and I, live the life of Libertines; for he takes his pleasure, and I take mine: Have you sent for Mr. Courtly?

2ND LADY
Yes, there are at least half a score Messengers sent one after another to invite him hither.

[Enter **MONSIEUR COURTLY**.

LADY AMOROUS
O Sir! you're welcome, we were even now a wishing for you to go abroad with us.

MONSIEUR COURTLY
I account my self happy, Ladies, that I am come according to your wishes, as also to do you service.

1ST LADY
We did send a dozen Messengers for you.

MONSIEUR COURTLY
I did happily meet them, Madam.

1ST LADY
But whether shall we go?

MONSIEUR COURTLY
Where you please, Lady; for I am ready at your service.

2ND LADY
Let us go to the Great Park.

LADY AMOROUS
No, let us go to the Fruit-Garden.

2ND LADY
No faith, upon better Consideration, let us stay and play at Cards.

LADY AMOROUS
That is dull; rather let us send for Fidlers, and Dance.

1ST LADY
We have not Men enough to dance, and Mr. Courtly cannot dance with us all.

MONSIEUR COURTLY

I'le do my endeavour, Ladies.

2ND LADY
No, let us hire a Barge, and row upon the Water.

LADY AMOROUS
No, let us go and Sup at the Tavern at the Bridg-foot; what say you, Mr. Courtly, will you entertain us?

MONSIEUR COURTLY
Yes, Lady, as well as I can.

1ST LADY
Let us go.

2ND LADY
No, let us first draw lots, and let Fortune decide the place of our Recreations.

LADY AMOROUS
Content; but which lot shall carry it?

1ST LADY
The long lot.

2ND LADY
The short lot.

1ST LADY
I say the long lot.

LADY AMOROUS
Let the most Voices carry it.

MONSIEUR COURTLY
Ladies, if I might perswade you, it should be at the Tavern at the Bridg-foot, and there you shall have the best Meat, Wine and Musick, that place affords.

OMNES
Content, content.

[Exeunt.

SCENE IV

[Enter **MONSIEUR FACIL** and **MONSIEUR ADVISER**.

MONSIEUR ADVISER

Facil, how do you prosper in Loves Adventures?

MONSIEUR FACIL
More happily then I could imagine, for she receives my Letters, and returns me Answers.

MONSIEUR ADVISER
Then you shall not need to despair, since you have such encouragement.

MONSIEUR FACIL
No faith, for now I fear she will be kinder then I would have her; for she has consented to a private meeting.

[Enter **MONSIEUR TAKE-PLEASURE** as in hast.

MONSIEUR ADVISER
Whether away in such hast, Tom?

MONSIEUR TAKE-PLEASURE
Faith, Courtly has sent his Footman to me in such hast, as the poor fellow is almost melted with the heat he has with running, to bring me a note from his Master, who writes to me, that of all love and friendship I should speedily come to him, and to bring half a dozen other Gentlemen with me to the Tavern, to help him to entertain a Company of Ladies, otherwise he shall die in their service; wherefore, prithee Adviser, and Facil, go with me thither.

MONSIEUR FACIL
Faith, we cannot, for we have other business.

MONSIEUR TAKE-PLEASURE
The same answer I have had from a dozen other Gentlemen, and cannot perswade any one to go; wherefore, I fear my friend Courtly will be over-power'd by those many Ladies.

MONSIEUR ADVISER
Why would Courtly engage himself to so many Women?

MONSIEUR TAKE-PLEASURE
Alas, he could not help it; for they sent so many Messengers to desire him to come to them, as he was almost smother'd in the croud, so that he was forced as it were, to go out in his own defence; but he finds that the Company of Ladies is worse then the number of Messengers, for he hath leaped out of the Frying-pan into the fire.

MONSIEUR ADVISER
I confess Men can hardly avoid the Females, and are more tormented with them then Beggars are with Lice, or a Horse with Flies; for since the Wars, numbers of Women do swarm about one Man, as Bees about a honey-pot.

MONSIEUR TAKE-PLEASURE
I confess it, and I fear my Friend Courtly will be devoured; wherefore, for Charity, go with me, and help him in distress, and I'le engage that he and I will do the like for either, or both of you.

MONSIEUR ADVISER
Upon that condition we are content; then let us go with all speed

[Exeunt.

[Enter **SIR MERCURY POET** to the **LADY FANCY**, whom He finds Weeping.

SIR MERCURY POET
Sweet Mistress! let not our Parents folly
Be a cause to make us Melancholy:
For Natures, Fates, and mighty gods above
Did make, Decree, and cause our Souls to love;
Then do not mourn, or cloud your Eyes with Tears,
But banish from your Mind all Griefs and Fears;
For still our Loving Souls will constant be,
Coelestial powers have joyn'd in that Decree.

LADY FANCY
But at full Moon, the winds blow high,
And in the wain they silent lie.
So doth a Lover's full griev'd Mind
Cause storms of Passions, like as Wind,
Beating the Thoughts, like Clouds about,
Which being prest, Tears streameth out.

SIR MERCURY POET
But when that Grief is in the wain
The Mind is smooth, and calm again;
Thoughts are serene, Joy shineth clear;
The Eyes are fair, no Tears appear:
But if that you with me consent,
Our Parents follies we'l prevent
With holy Ceremony, bind so sure
In Sacred Marriage, shall for life endure.

LADY FANCY
I do consent to be your Wife.
For without you, I have no Life.

[Exeunt.

SCENE V

[Enter **SIR WILLIAM SAGE**, **LADY VERTUE**, and **MIMICK**.

SIR WILLIAM SAGE
What are you studying your Play?

MIMICK
Yes faith, I am getting some speeches by heart.

SIR WILLIAM SAGE
Let us hear some of them.

MIMICK
I cannot speak like a Woman in Breeches and Doublet, unless I have a Petticoat.

[Enter the **COOK-MAID**.

MAID
Madam, I come to know what shall be drest for Supper?

MIMICK
My Lady will fast and pray to night; wherefore, lend me one of thy Petticoats.

MAID
What will you do with it?

MIMICK
I'le not eat thy Petticoat, though it would fry in its own grease, but I would use it another way.

MAID
What other way?

MIMICK
Why, I will wear thy Petticoat over my Breeches.

MAID
No, by my Faith, but you shall not; for then my Petticoat and your Breeches may commit Fornication.

MIMICK
It were better our Clothes should commit Fornication, then our Persons; but in my Conscience our Clothes will be honest; but it is probable, that the Fleas in your Petticoat, and the Fleas in my Breeches may commit Fornication; and so our Clothes, or rather our selves will be guilty of another such like Vertue, as Fornication; which is, I shall be a Pimp, and you a Bawd for the Adulterous Fleas; but howsoever I must borrow thy Petticoat.

MAID
Would you have me lend you my Petticoat, and stand my self naked?

MIMICK

If you should, it would seem a deed of Charity, to give thy Petticoat from off thee, to those that want it; besides, you will appear like the Picture of Eve in her state of Innocence; and when I have done acting my part, of seeming a Woman, I will be like Adam; and so we shall be both like our first Parents.

MAID
I'le see you hang'd in an Apple-tree, before I lend you my Petticoat.

MIMICK
Then I shall not need it, unless it be for a shroud to lap me in; but rather then you will see me hang'd, you will cut the cord or halter, although you were sure to damn your Soul for the deed; but if thou wilt lend me thy Petticoat, I will promise hereafter to be thy Champion Knight, armed with thy Kitchin-Vessels; thy Spit shall be my long Sword or Tuck, and thy Dripping-pan my Target, thy Porridg-pot my Head-piece, one of thy Pie-plates shall serve for a breast-plate, and a Buff-coat made of the smuddy skins of Gammons of Bacon.

MAID
Upon that condition, to see you so armed, I will lend you my upper-Petticoat, if my Master and Lady will give me leave.

MIMICK
Thou hast their leave; for I must act my part for them to see me; and I had rather wear thy upper-Coat, then thy under-Petticoat.

[She pulls off her Petticoat.

LADY VERTUE
Joan, help him to put it on.

MIMICK
No, I will put it on my self, for she will put it over my head, and I will put it under my feet, for I had rather my feet should go thorough her Petticoat, then my nose should be in her tayl, which will be, if I put her Petticoat over my head.

[She snatches her Petticoat away.

MAID
You jeering Fool, you shall not have my Petticoat to play the Fool with.

MIMICK
You Slut, take your Coat again, for the smell makes me sick, and suffocates my breath.

MAID
You are a lying fellow, for saying my Petticoat stinks.

MIMICK
Prithee Joan, be pacified; for I confess, my smell is a foolish, nice, sickly smell; but for thy comfort, many right Honourable, and right noble Persons love the haut-goust of such Petticoats; but the perfume of thy

Petticoat, has spoiled the part of my Play; for it hath put me quite out of the Amorous Speeches, I should have rehears'd.

SIR WILLIAM SAGE

But it is not so proper for a Woman to speak Amorous Speeches, as for a Man; wherefore, speak some Amorous Speeches to Joan, as a Man in your own Garments.

MIMICK

But my Speech was to be spoken in the absence of my Lover; complaining to the gods, and imploring their favours to assist me to the sight of my Love.

SIR WILLIAM SAGE

That would have been rather as a Prayer, then an Amorous Speech.

MIMICK

No, no, I would have order'd my Speech so as it should have been Amorous.

LADY VERTUE

Then I perceive we shall hear none of your Play at this time.

MIMICK

I have parts to act as a Man; which is to address my sels in a Courtly manner to some fine, fair, sweet, young Lady.

LADY VERTUE

Imagine Joan such a Lady.

MIMICK

My Imagination is not so powerful, as to Metamorphose Joan in my Thoughts to such a Lady; besides, Joan cannot answer a Man as she should.

MAID

You lie, you Rogue, for I have answer'd better men then thou art, or ever wilt be.

MIMICK

But can you talk Court-talks?

MAID

I know not what Court-talk is, but I can talk.

MIMICK

Stand forth here, and I will court thee as a Gallant doth his Mistress: Lady, your Beauty shines.

MAID

That is, because I wash'd it with some of the Beef-broth, and wiped it with a greasie clout, I use to wipe the dishes; otherwise, the great hot shining fire i'th' Kitchin would burn and parch it so dry, as it would be scurvy, or scabby.

MIMICK

Setting aside your basted, rosted face, I must tell you, it is not the Courtly manner to interrupt a Man in his speech; you must be silent until the end of the Speech, and then speak; but you spoke when I had not said above four words: hold your peace, and I'le begin again. Lady, your Beauty shineth like a blazing-Star, whereon Men gaze, and in their Minds do wonder at the sight; but the effects are not alike; your Beauty strikes them not with fear, but Love; your frowns and smiles are Destiny and Fate, either to kill or cure.

MAID

What Language is this, French or Dutch, or Welch, or Irish, or Scotch!

MIMICK

No, it is Greek and Hebrew.

MAID

Speak to me so, as I may understand you; otherwise, I cannot answer you.

MIMICK

Joan, thy face shines like a Sea-coal fire.

MAID

Why, doth it look red?

MIMICK

Faith, thy Nose appears like a burning coal, rak'd over with black ashes, but all thy face else appears like the outside of a roasted Pig.

MAID

You are a roasted Ass, for saying my face appears like the outside of a roasted Pig; my face is a face of God's own making, and not a Pig's face.

MIMICK

No, I know your face is a Sow's face; but I say the colour of your face is like the Coat of a roasted Pig.

MAID

My face is as good a face as your own, without any dispraise to the party.

MIMICK

Which party? the Fools party, or the Sluts party?

MAID

Well, for saying my face is like a Pig's Coat, i'faith when I roast a Pig again, you shall not have any part of it; and let me give you warning, you come not into the Kitchin; for if you do, I will fling a Ladle full of Drippings upon your Fools Coat.

[Exit **MAID**.

MIMICK

O wo is me! I shall lose many a hot bit; but Master and Lady, this is your fault to make Joan and I fall out.

LADY VERTUE
We did not make you fall out.

MIMICK
You commanded me to Court Joan, and she doth not understand Courtships in words; for Joan is used to be kiss'd, and not wooed; but I will go and promise Joan a kiss, although I never pay it her; for the more hungry she is, the better she'l feed me.

[Exeunt.

ACT V

SCENE I

[Enter **MONSIEUR FACIL, MONSIEUR ADVISER,** and **MONSIEUR TAKE-PLEASURE.**

MONSIEUR TAKE-PLEASURE
Facil, I am come to fetch thee to the Horn-Tavern, for there be a number of Good-fellows that want thy Company.

MONSIEUR FACIL
Stay, stay; I must go and make a Cuckold first.

MONSIEUR TAKE-PLEASURE
Thou hast made a Hundred in thy time.

MONSIEUR FACIL
But I must go and make one to day; for I am going to meet a young beautiful Wife in private.

MONSIEUR TAKE-PLEASURE
Put off thy Meeting until another time.

MONSIEUR FACIL
That I cannot, I am so engaged; besides, she is a Lady of Honour.

MONSIEUR ADVISER
Of Title you mean; for Ladies of Honour, or Honourable Ladies, do not use to have private Meetings with such wild deboist Men as thou art; and if she be a Wife, as you say she is, it will be no great honour for her Husband.

MONSIEUR FACIL
You speak as if you were a Married Man, and were sensible of a Husbands disgrace.

MONSIEUR ADVISER

The truth is, I find I have a Commiseration and Compassion for Married Men.

MONSIEUR FACIL
But not when you are to lie with any of their Wives.

MONSIEUR ADVISER
I seldom make love to Married Wives; for they are not worth the trouble and danger which a Man must pass through before they can be enjoyed; besides, a Man loses a great deal of time in Wooing them, not but that they are as yielding, nay, more yielding then Maids; but they are more fearful to venture, lest their Husbands should know it.

MONSIEUR FACIL
Faith, Maids are more troublesome and chargable then Wives; for they are apt to claim Marriage, or to sue for maintenance at least; besides, their lying in, and Christening, breeding and bringing up of their Children, is an intollerable Charge; which charge is sav'd with Married Wives; and for their Husbands, they are contented to wink, not willing to see their disgraces, at least not to divulge them.

MONSIEUR ADVISER
Not all; for some will look with more eyes then their own, setting spies to watch them.

MONSIEUR FACIL
Those are old-fashioned Husbands, and not Mode-Husbands.

MONSIEUR ADVISER
Indeed, I observe, that Mode-Husbands do not love their Wives, unless other Men Court them; and if your Mistress's Husband is such a one, you shall not need to meet in private.

MONSIEUR FACIL
I think my Mistress's Husband is not so much of the French fashion, although my Mistress is Frenchified.

MONSIEUR TAKE-PLEASURE
What, has she the French Pox?

MONSIEUR FACIL
I hope not; for Ladies of her Quality have not that foul infectious Disease; but I mean my Mistress is in the French Fashion, not in the French Disease: But farwell, for I must be gone; otherwise, I shall slip my time.

MONSIEUR TAKE-PLEASURE
Prithee go along with me.

MONSIEUR FACIL
I'le leave you, my friend here; for my self I must go, otherwise I should prove my self a Fool, to lose the time I have spent in Wooing, the Money I have given in bribing, the Sleeps I have mist with watching, the Protestations and Vows I have made in swearing, and my word that is past in promising, if I should not meet her and enjoy her; but when I am parted from her, I will come to you.

MONSIEUR TAKE-PLEASURE

Well, I am content to spare thee so long; for I would not have thee a loser, although my faith tells me, you will not gain much: But remember the meeting at the Horn-Tavern.

MONSIEUR FACIL
I shall not forget that sign of any sign; wherefore, doubt not of my Company.

[Exeunt.

[Enter **LADY VERTUE** and **MIMICK**.

LADY VERTUE
Mimick, to my sight you appear dull, since you are Married!

MIMICK
Faith, I do not find my self so lively as I was before I Married; for a Wife is a clog to a Man's heels, and a cloud in a Man's mind; but your Ladyship seems more lively since you were Married, then you did before.

LADY
The reason is,
That a good Husband is a light to a Woman's life, a friend to a Woman's Vertue, and a Crown to a Woman's honour.

MIMICK
And an ill Wife is a Horn to a Man's head, a Plague to a Man's life, and a death to a Man's wit.

LADY
Indeed your Mimick -Wit seems dead since you Married; but yet my Maid Nan, whom you Married, is a good Wife.

MIMICK
Yes, when she is in a good humor.

LADY
Let me advise you to return to your Mimick-humour, or I will tell your Wife, that you repent your Marriage.

MIMICK
She may perceive that by my cold kindness; howsoever, I'le live like a Batchellor, although I am a Married Man.

LADY
How can you do so?

MIMICK
Why, I will live Chast.

LADY
That will be well for Nan

[Enter **SIR WILLIAM SAGE**.

SIR WILLIAM SAGE
Wife, I have invited some Strangers to dine with me to morrow; wherefore, I would have you dress your self fine to entertain them.

LADY
If you like me in plain Garments as well as in rich, I care not how Strangers like me.

SIR WILLIAM SAGE
I would have my Wife appear so handsome to Strangers, as they may approve of my Choice.

LADY
Some Men would be afraid if their Wives should be seen by Strangers, least they might like so well their Choice, as to chuse them for their Mistresses.

SIR WILLIAM SAGE
But my Wife's Vertue makes me fearless of Strangers.

LADY
But Vertue is not proved, until it be tryed.

SIR WILLIAM SAGE
True love is never inconstant.

LADY
But true love is not known until it be tryed.

SIR WILLIAM SAGE
I fear not a trial.

LADY
But a trial of Chastity is scandalous; for Overberry in his Characters says,
That he comes not near, that comes to be denied.

SIR WILLIAM SAGE
Then I will entertain the Strangers, and keep you in your Chamber.

LADY
I shall so.

MIMICK

Madam, my Master having Strangers to morrow, pray let me add one dish to the Feast.

SIR WILLIAM SAGE
What Dish is that, a dress'd Lady?

MIMICK
No; for my skill in Physick doth plainly prove, that Ladies are unwholsome meat, they will give a Man a Surfeit; besides, they are not tastable, unless they be very tender and young; also, they are very chargable in dressing, they require so many Ingrediences and garnishings to set them off, and so much sauce to make them relish well, as would undo a poor Man; besides, much art is required in the Dressing: So all considered, they are not worth the charge, labour and time, being but a faint, weak and sickly meat at the best, but I have thought of other meat, which will be tastable meat to a great Monarch.

SIR WILLIAM SAGE
What meat is that?

MIMICK
An Hodge-podge.

SIR WILLIAM SAGE
It seems it is for a Dutch Monarch; but let us know how you will make it?

MIMICK
First, I will take Widows dissembling Tears, Maids dissembling Modesty, Wives dissembling Chastity, Curtisans dissembling Virginity, Puritanical Sisters dissembling Piety, Autumnal Ladies dissembling Beauty; and mixing all these Ingrediences together, I will put them into a Mystical pot, and set it on a heatless fiery Meteor a stewing, and after it has stew'd some time, I'le put these Ingrediences to them, The Pride of Favourites, the Vanity of Courtiers, the Jugling of Statesmen, the Fears of Cowards, the mischiefs of Tumults, the Extortion of Magistrates, the Covetousness of Usurers, the Retards of Judges, the Quirks of Lawyers, the Opiniateness of Schollars, the Jealousie of Lovers, the Deceit of Tradesmen, the Brags of Soldiers, the Oaths of Gamesters, the Prodigality of young Heirs, the Diseases of Drunkards, the Surfeits of Gluttons, and the dishonour of Cuckolds; Likewise, I will put in a Fool's Brain, a Liers Tongue, a Traiterous Heart, and a Thieves Had; With which I'le stir all together, and after they have been well stew'd and stir'd together, I'le take this Hodg-podg and put it into a large dish of Infamy, and garnish it with the dotgae of Age, the follies of Youth, the superstition of Idolaters, and the expectation of Chymists, and then serve it up to Pluto 's Table.

LADY
For once I will try my Huswifry to Cook a dish of meat, which shall be a Bisk: First, I will take the Truth of Religion, the Piety of Saints, the Chastity of Nunns, the Purity of Virginity, the Constancy of true Love, the Unity of Friendship, the Innocency of Infants, the Wit of Poets, the Eloquence of Orators, the Learning of Scholars, the Valour of Soldiers, the Knowledg of Travellers, and Time's Experience; And put all these into a pot of Renown, and set it on a Coelestial fire a stewing; after it has stew'd some time, I'le put in these Ingredients, Wholsome Temperance, strengthning Fortitude, comfortable Justice, and savory Prudence; also, I'le add the bowels of Compassion, the Heart of Honesty, the Brain of Wisdom, the Tongue of Truth, and the Hand of Generosity; and stir them well together, then I'le take them off, and put them into a dish of Happiness, and garnish it with the Plenty of Prosperity, the Ease of Rest, the

Delight of Beauty, and the Tranquillity of Peace, and so serve it up to Jove 's Table. Thus I am a Cook-maid for the gods; but you are a Cook-man for the Devil, and all the meat you Cook, is burnt.

MIMICK

I confess, Hell's fire is great and scorching, and Hell's Kitchin is very hot; but howsoever, my Master the Devil loves his meat thoroughly roasted, and tenderly stew'd; but your Master Jove loves all his meat cold and raw; for there is not any fire in Heaven, and that is the reason you chuse to be a Servant to the gods; because you would not burn your face, lest it should spoile your Complexion; for Ladies are more careful of their Faces then their Souls; besides, the cool and temperate air, and the cold diet of the gods, which breeds flegm, makes them patient; whereas, the Devil is dwelling in a Torrid Region, and eating dry roasted meat, which breeds Choller, makes him furious; in so much, as he tortures his Servants with grievous pains.

LADY

Why do you serve him then?

MIMICK

Because, he gives great wages; I serve him for necessity, but some serve him for worldly honour, and some for worldly wealth, and some for worldly power, and some for one thing, and some for another; for none serves him for love, neither do the Servants of the gods serve them for love but for some reward.

SIR WILLIAM SAGE

Let me perswade you to change your Service.

MIMICK

So I will, when I am old, and can serve the Devil no longer, then I will leave his Service, and serve the gods.

SIR WILLIAM SAGE

But the gods will not then accept of your Service.

MIMICK

But they will; for the gods refuse not any that offer their service; The truth is, the gods cannot get Servants enough to serve them, so as they are forced to take any that will but serve them; for the gods have but the Devils leavings and refusals, as those that are so old as to be past sin; or so sickly, as they cannot act sin; or those that are so young, as not to know sin; for most of the gods Servants are aged and weak persons, or young Children.

SIR WILLIAM SAGE

I perceive you will wear out sin, before you serve the gods.

MIMICK

No, sin shall wear out me, before I serve them.

LADY

You are a sinful Rogue.

MIMICK
All Mankind is so, more or less, even your Lordship; the gods bless you, and have mercy upon you.

LADY
Well, to punish you for your Sins, you shall eat no other meat but what your Poetical Fancy dresses.

MIMICK
I shall be starved then.

[Exeunt.

SCENE III

[Enter **MONSIEUR COURTLY**, and **MONSIEUR ADVISER**.

MONSIEUR ADVISER
Courtly! 'tis strange to see you in this humour, as dying for the love of one Woman, when as I thought you had taken a surfeit of all Womenkind!

MONSIEUR COURTLY
'Tis true, I have Courted some Women, and many Women have Courted me; but I did never truly love any Woman but this Woman, which I cannot enjoy.

MONSIEUR ADVISER
Have you no hopes to linger your life a little time longer?

MONSIEUR COURTLY
Faith, I believe my life will continue, but my hopes are buried in despair.

MONSIEUR ADVISER
If you had but the opportunity to Court this Lady, you are so madly in love with, at any time, I am confident you may gain her good will; for Women are as various in their denials and consentings to their Lovers, as they are in their fashions and garments; for they will love and hate, and hate and love one and the same, many several times; as now love, then hate, now hate, then love; for Ladies affections change like the Seasons, or the Weather, as sometimes hot, and sometimes cold, and sometimes luke-warm.

MONSIEUR COURTLY
The affections of the Lady I love, are at all times cold, even to numness; for she is insensible towards me, and to all Lovers else, for any thing I can perceive.

MONSIEUR ADVISER
Is she such a frozen Lady?

MONSIEUR COURTLY

Yes faith; for I think she is composed of Ice, or a statue made of Snow.

MONSIEUR ADVISER
If she be composed of Ice or Snow, I dare assure you, she may be melted.

MONSIEUR COURTLY
How?

MONSIEUR ADVISER
Why, be you in the Torrid Zone of Mode, in Speech, Behaviour and Accoustrements, and let your Garments be so rich, as to shine in Gold and Silver, whose glistering rayes will cast a glorious splendor; then address your self in Poetical flames, and being a hot Lover, you will thaw her into your arms, and melt her unto your desire: Thus a Western Lover, and a Northern Lady may meet in Conjunction together.

MONSIEUR COURTLY
But cold Chastity has congealed and crystallined this Lady, in so much, as the hottest Lover with all his Poetical flames, and splenderous rayes of Youth, Beauty, Title, Wealth or Bravery, has not power to change or alter her worth and honour; for like a durable Diamond she is, and will remain.

MONSIEUR ADVISER
Who is the Owner of this rich Jewel?

MONSIEUR COURTLY
Sir W. Sage, who is a wise, valiant man, and will not part from her, nor suffer any Man to take her from him; for he wears her in his heart, and she is the delight of his Life, and the Crown of his Honour, in which he takes more Glory, pride and pleasure, then to be Crowned Emperor of the whole World.

MONSIEUR ADVISER
He hath reason; for a Man may sooner conquer the World, then find such another Chast Woman as she is.

MONSIEUR COURTLY
Well, since I cannot obtain my desire, I will travel.

MONSIEUR ADVISER
That is the best for you to do, for so you may tire out Love.

MONSIEUR COURTLY
Or Love tire out me.

MONSIEUR ADVISER
Faith, you are tir'd out of Courtship, and if you can tire out Love, you will do well; but before you go to Travel, you must go to a dancing-meeting of Ladies and Gentlemen.

[Exeunt.

[Enter **MR LONG-LIFE**, and **MR AGED**.

MR AGED

Mr. Longlife, I am come to tell you, That your Son Mercury hath stoln away my Daughter Fancy, and as I hear, they are gone to Apollo 's Church to be Married.

MR LONG-LIFE

Mr. Aged, I am sorry for it, and wish he had stoln a Challenge, when he stole your Daughter.

MR AGED

And I wish my Daughter had Married an Ass, rather then Marry your Son.

MR LONG-LIFE

Well, if they be Married, as sure they are, if they have any Children we will endeavour to breed them Fools.

MR AGED

We will so.

[Enter the **MARRIED COUPLE**: They kneel down.

SIR MERCURY POET

We desire your Blessing.

MR LONG-LIFE

Well, since you are Married, God bless you; But Son and Daughter in Law, I desire and command yon in the name of a Father, that you will leave Versifying, Rhyming, Similizing, and the like, but study the Politicks, and that will abate your Wit.

MR AGED

They may study Virgils Georgicks, for that treats of good Husbandry.

MR LONG-LIFE

Yes, brother Aged, but it is in Verse, and whatsoever they get in Husbandry, they will lose by the Rhyme.

MR AGED

By the Mass you say true, Brother Longlife.

MR LONG-LIFE

Well Brother, although they have Married against our consent, yet we will celebrate their Marriage with Feasting, Mirth, and Musick.

SIR MERCURY POET

Musick Sir, is a part of Poetry, and belongs to the Muses.

MR LONG-LIFE

Yes, yes, but not such Musick as we will have, two or three Scraping Fidlers, that plays neither tune nor time.

[Enter the Lady Fancy as a Bride, and Sir Mercury Poet as Bridegroom; and all the Ladies and Gentlemen that were Guests at the first Wedding.

MR AGED
Brother Longlife, we are not for these active sports, our dancing-days are done.

MR LONG-LIFE
You say true, brother Aged; but in our younger years we were as agil as the best of them all.

[A **YOUNG LADY** takes out **MR LONG-LIFE** to dance.

LADY
Sir, although you be old, you may walk a grave measure, as a Paven.

MR LONG-LIFE
Say you so, my Girl; and i'faith I will try what my old legs will do; here brother Aged you shall hold my staff whil'st I dance.

MR AGED
Nay, b'r'lady, your staff brother Longlife will help to prop up your weakness; and since a young Lady hath chose you to dance with, I will chuse out a Lady to dance with me; but the Musicians must play slow, or we shall not keep time; wherefore, Musicians let not your Fiddles go faster then our Legs, nor your Tunes to be younger then our years, but an old Paven.

[The **OLD MEN** dance with **TWO YOUNG LADIES**, they dance softly, but right, and keep time.

[The **YOUNG SMILE** smile.

MR AGED
You young Men smile, but we could have danced as nimbly as you can now.

SIR MERCURY POET
You will teach us a sober pace, Sir.

MR LONG-LIFE
No Son, Time must teach you that, to which we will leave you, and my Brother and I will rest our Legs whil'st you tire your Legs: Come brother Aged, let us leave them to their Mirth, Musick, and Youth.

MARGARET CAVENDISH – A CONCISE BIBLIOGRAPHY

Philosophical Fancies (1653)
Poems and Fancies (1653)
Philosophical and Physical Opinions (1655)
Nature's Pictures drawn by Fancie's Pencil to the Life (1656)
The World's Olio (1655)
Playes, (1662) folio, containing twenty-one plays including

Loves Adventures
The Several Wits
Youths Glory, and Deaths Banquet
The Lady Contemplation
Wits Cabal
The Unnatural Tragedy
The Public Wooing
The Matrimonial Trouble
Nature's Three Daughters (Beauty, Love and Wit) Part I & Part II
The Religious
The Comical Hash
Bell in Campo
A Comedy of the Apocryphal Ladies
The Female Academy
Plays never before printed (1668), containing five plays.
The Sociable Companions, or the Female Wits
The Presence
The Bridals
The Convent of Pleasure
A Piece of a Play
Orations of Divers Sorts (1662)
Philosophical Letters, or Modest Reflections upon some Opinions in Natural Philosophy maintained by several learned authors of the age (1664)
CCXI Sociable Letters (1664)
Observations upon Experimental Philosophy & Description of a New World (1666)
The Blazing World (1666)
The Life of William Cavendish, Duke, Marquis, and Earl of Newcastle, Earl of Ogle, Viscount Mansfield, and Baron of Bolsover, of Ogle, Bothal, and Hepple, &c. (1667)
Grounds of Natural Philosophy (1668)

www.ingramcontent.com/pod-product-compliance
Lightning Source LLC
Chambersburg PA
CBHW021941040426
42448CB00008B/1186